This delightful book is the latest in the series of Ladybird books that have been specially planned to help grown-ups with the world about them.

As in the other books in this series, the large, clear script, the careful choice of words, the frequent repetition and the thoughtful matching of text with pictures all enable grown-ups to think they have taught themselves to cope. The subject of the book will greatly appeal to grown-ups.

Series 999

THE LADYBIRD
BOOKS FOR GROWN-UPS SERIES

DATING

by

J. A. HAZELEY, N.S.F.W. and J. P. MORRIS, O.M.G.

(Authors of 'Lose Weight With Extreme Shaving')

Publishers: Ladybird Books Ltd, Loughborough
Printed in England. If wet, Italy.

Dating is a fun way of meeting someone who is as terrified of dying alone as you are.

Finding this person takes time. Cupid's arrow can strike when you least expect.

Angela has been struck by Cupid's arrow, and is going to live happily ever after.

Lonely people know "the one" is out there somewhere. They will search the whole world for them.

It is surprising how often that soul-mate turns out to not be on the other side of the world, but fairly nearby, and reasonably drunk.

The perfect match.

Men's brains and women's brains are different, even as children.

Boys like to knock a Hula Hoop off an After Eight with a cocktail stick. Girls prefer balancing a first-class stamp on top of a Mr Man's bowler hat.

To get along, men and women pretend not to mind those little differences.

Or they become homosexuals.

Finding time for love is hard because modern people have busy lives.

Pat runs an artisanal macaroon business. She has been very busy.

One day she notices she has forgotten to get married and still sleeps on a mattress on the floor.

Time is running out for Pat.

Dating is all about meeting new people.

Alex spends the whole day at work. Once an hour, he meets the same person, his supervisor, Tim.

Tim asks Alex how many funnels there are now. Alex tells him. Alex gets home late and falls asleep in front of a programme about vans.

Alex does not meet new people.

Deborah has had many, many unsuccessful dates in the last eight years and still cannot find Mr Right.

Her friends tell her she should lower her expectations. Deborah is trying her very best.

She still would prefer her dream man to have wings or a crown, but he no longer needs to be literally made of gold.

Getting ready is part of the date. Michelle's friend Allanah has been doing Michelle's hair since Wednesday.

Michelle's date, Chris, is still at home. He has prepared by doing up most of the buttons on his shirt, and tidying his fringe with spit.

He is finishing a mission on Call of Duty and will be twenty minutes late.

Vanessa is meeting Callum for their first date.

To help spot each other, Callum and Vanessa have both agreed to wear red. Callum said he would wear his uniform from work.

Vanessa was very excited. She thought that Callum might be a guardsman.

Lynn has come to a record discothèque. She is hoping to meet a new person to spend the rest of her life with again.

The loud music makes the new people impossible to talk to. Luckily, alcohol means what they are saying is unlikely to be important or interesting.

"Four hundredth time lucky," thinks Lynn.

Bernard and Gail are on-line friends who have finally met. They know they have a lot in common and are going for a walk.

All Bernard can think about is checking his telephone. All Gail can think about is how she is going to describe this date in 140 characters later when she goes to the toilet.

Bernard and Gail suspect that in real life they are simply awful people.

Andrew has said fewer than eleven words during his date with Lionel. Lionel eats quickly.

"I should be going," says Lionel.

"Don't go," says Andrew. "This is the best date I've had all year."

"But my plate is empty," says Lionel.

"Finish the salt. Then we can go," says Andrew.

Lionel and Andrew eat the salt.

Vernon is on a first date with Frances. He has chosen a venue he frequents regularly where he feels comfortable and can be himself.

Because Vernon is relaxed, Frances is relaxed too. The date is going well.

Frances is glad they did not go to the Wetherspoon's.

Phil has arranged to meet Abigail in a basement wine bar.

The bar is hot and Phil is not used to drinking red wine. His shirt was off before the bruschetta arrived and he has challenged the waiter to a sword fight.

Abigail is going to give it half an hour and call a cab.

It might be only a one-night-stand, but there is still room for romance.

Gregory has spent the night in a public bomb shelter with Pam.

In the morning, he surprises her with a cup of tea and a Bruce Forsyth impersonator.

Malcolm and Trina are on a date they both can enjoy — buying a new calendar. They both love dates. And also love dates.

Malcolm and Trina are calendar buffs. They met at a local calendar club and have a lot in common.

The only argument is over which date they are going to pick for their next date — because they love them all!

Neeta is moving into Owen's flat. Commitment makes Owen nervous.

"One step at a time," says Neeta.

At the garden centre, Neeta suggests buying a lawn ornament to mark their new life as a couple.

"This one looks nice," says Neeta.

David and Penelope are buying a jar of lemon curd, which they plan to eat this evening over a game of Hungry Hippos.

"My girlfriend will pay," says David.

Penelope smiles. David has never called her his girlfriend before. The grocer smiles too.

"Look at my girlfriend like that again," says David, "and I'll break your legs."

Rebecca is meeting Ian for their fifth date. But Ian has not come. Rebecca is sad.

Ian sends a text message instead. He says he is under too much pressure from Rebecca, who is "calling him everyday".

Rebecca thinks this is a lucky escape.

"Every day" is two words.

Frank divorced three years ago. Frank's friend Geoff says Frank should start dating again.

Frank is out of practice. He does not like where Geoff goes to meet partners.

"This place is a cattle market," says Frank.

Geoff says Frank is not seeing the potential. Geoff got off with an auctioneer here last week.

Marcus and Fiona have had three dates.

Fiona knows this means she will either end up spending the rest of her life with Marcus, or eventually have to break up with him, horribly.

Both of these ideas are terrifying to Fiona.

Tomorrow Fiona will fake her own death and join Cirque du Soleil.

Judith is breaking up with Tony. She knows a text message can be impersonal so she has come to her local Post Office.

The lady at the counter checks Judith's envelope is sealed. If any of the faeces leaks out, the Post Office is not obliged to carry it.

Judith sends her package by recorded delivery. She can make sure it has reached Tony and know she is single again.

In other countries, dating is very different.

Boleg has four good beetroot fields. Yogóp and Iomog have claimed him.

This evening the women will fight to the death using traditional hammers.

In the morning the winner will marry, mate with, and eat Boleg.

In the future, dating may be very different.

Zaqary is offworlding the data for a new relationship on to his leisure cloud, to enjoy later.

He has chosen e-dinner with his administrator Egmilon.

Here in the year 4,000,000,000, workplace romance is forbidden. But Egmilon and Zaqary's avatars can marry, as long as they have a five-star user rating.

It is Barney and Leigh's wedding day. They have certainly come a long way from their first date.

They have learned to suppress their personalities and pretend they want the same things, so they will be able to put up with each other for several years.

Everyone is happy for them.

Their story is over.

THE AUTHORS would like to record their gratitude and offer their apologies to the many Ladybird artists whose luminous work formed the glorious wallpaper of countless childhoods. Revisiting it for this book as grown-ups has been a privilege.

MICHAEL JOSEPH

UK | USA | Canada | Ireland | Australia
India | New Zealand | South Africa

Michael Joseph is part of the Penguin Random House group of companies whose addresses can be found at global.penguinrandomhouse.com
First published 2015

010

Text copyright © Jason Hazeley and Joel Morris, 2015
All images copyright © Ladybird Books Ltd, 2015

The moral right of the authors has been asserted

Printed in Italy by L.E.G.O. S.p.A

A CIP catalogue record for this book is available from the British Library

ISBN: 978–0–718–18357–8

www.greenpenguin.co.uk

MIX
Paper from
responsible sources
FSC® C018179
www.fsc.org

Penguin Random House is committed to a sustainable future for our business, our readers and our planet. This book is made from Forest Stewardship Council® certified paper.